# THE RAZOR'S EDGE

# The Razor's Edge

James Street

**To order additional copies of this book, contact:**
Xlibris
844-714-8691
www.Xlibris.com
Orders@Xlibris.com
830420

For Laura, Kevin, Mike, and Devon. Your light
feeds mine. I appreciate you deeply.

I'm the man with many names,
but for now, just call me James.

# Contents

## SONG LYRICS

# THE QUIXOTIC MOLD

Devilish snare
erupts from your soul;
fit the quixotic mold.

Juniper tea
from the galley
to the gallows,
and it bubbles as you bellow.

Indigent song
leads you into the maze,
but the throngs soon
show you the way.

Your gaze
set upon a sea of faces,
and you say,
"Love is the answer"
or some such thing.
And buried inside,
the truth ever stings.

# CONSIDER THIS

Consider your hands.
Consider a grain of sand.
Consider the rushing water
in an erstwhile roaring canyon.
Now it quietly hums
while I,
beating the shaman's drum,
forge a new path
that has always existed.

The way,
as twisted
as all of existence,
coexists
with a force
that purports
to be the
truth.

I know the two roads
that diverge in a wood.
Structure and freedom,
those stubborn siblings,
both laying claim
to the holy land
that is man's
soul.

And both
laying blame
for our imperfections
on the other's weaknesses.

The soil,
once rich and fertile,
is beginning to turn
an arid, sickly beige.
Begging,
how do we unify
two distinct sides
without crucifying
the one
and calcifying
the mind?

# On the Forest Floor

So my feet are stained
permanently,
as I walk across the muddy plain
that gave birth to me.

And I build my house
of sticks and dirt,
that's fated
to crumble back to earth.
And each time it dies,
I raise my hands to the sky
and scream,
"Why is this happening to me!"

You're all here,
living with the fear.
You're all with me,
suffering interminably.

Then somebody speaks
of another place
where the sand is hot
and the sun is bright
and gold bricks lay in wait.

Hearing this,
each one sprints

away from here
to catch a glimpse
of endless golden years.

Then word comes back
to the forest firs
that a man has found
this heaven on earth.

He built his palace
made of gold
with dreams of never getting old.

His life is perfect,
but one thing's strange.
He's plagued with bouts
of acid rain.

And so
in my faulty forest
I remain.

# THE DEVIL HAS BLACK EYES

The devil has black eyes.
I went to his "meetings."
I stood with the mass of
blond-eyed, blue-haired lookers-on.
We shared a collective
gaze
as he told us how we
felt.

All is quiet
when the devil speaks,
save for the faint cackling of the
fire
from which no light emanates.
I curried favor with him.
I let him [redact my act]
as I cradled an infant song.
I listened
as he uttered words
of great power
but no meaning.

I stared into those eyes.
Those big black eyes.

The devil knows
*nothing.*
He is at the mercy of an indifferent cosmos.
I traveled to the black hole
behind his eyes
and abandoned my infant song.
This act
caused me a pain greater
than the devil could ever hope to comprehend.

Yes,
the devil is alive,
but he's changing.

# Asleep in My Dreams

It happened again,
so again I told myself it wouldn't happen again.
What was there to gain?
An ounce of pleasure?
A refrain of the most overplayed song in history.
I consider paying someone to write this drivel for me.
I,
who guarded time's secrets so well,
I lost not only them but myself.

There I lie,
dreaming of snakes and apples.
I bite
the apple.
Crisp, tart, sweet, and juicy;
it excites my palate.
And I wonder,
why must the weak manipulate the strong?
And where has the world's fucking dignity gone?

In 90 percent
of any given dream,
    you're asleep.
    Remember Me.

# My Mind

My mind,
trivialized in a sequence of
fair-weather fecundity.
Oh, what sunny days
do to me.
Let your inhibitions
marinate
in the fundament of your
mortal soul.

I've got all day.

I am your mirror
and
your maid of honor.
I squander
every opportunity
just to prove
my petty autonomy.

# The Word Was Quagmire

Single vein
pulsating
as the
pineal ping-pong match
progresses.
It's fucking stressful,
this parade of personas
playing charades
in a conga line.
One foot in the grave,
the other
toeing the line.
"Sorry," said the girl,
"I couldn't quite catch that."
Well, Ms. Elektra,
repetition is a bore,
and dignifying the lie
is a goddamn chore.

# Dirty Martini with a Twist

Lukewarm milk
with a gratuitous sprinkling of
cinnamon and cayenne
swishes in the
oblong bowl
with a thunderous thirst
to escape
the confines of the
eggshell environs.
The sirens
caw endlessly.
They mimic
the plodding quality
of the overbred animal
asserting its humanity.
As they prod you with
electric elocutions,
they push the panic button
further in your direction.

# REVOLUTIONS

Speckled glass
distorts the image
enough to remind us:
we are the actor
and the audience,
reactive and radiative.

Hanging glasses
bereft of function,
transforming light into shadow
with the jagged edge of artifice.

Consider your hand:
open,
soft spindles of dexterous flesh.
Balled into a fist,
now the tool of the orator,
generator of emotion.
Take this baneful boulder
from my chest.
Lover, lay me gently
now
to rest.

# Smells like Teenage Memories

Hidden referee,
surveying my past
at an eighty-nine-degree angle.
You whistle a muted melody
which mutates me
into seething melancholy.
O, pray, world,
forget my folly!
Let me start anew,
free from the chains of
reverberating thought waves.
The protagonist contemplated
Gatsby,
trying to good-will his way
out of karmic justice.
But the creeping past wasn't Gatsby's
downfall.
It was his belief that any of it
mattered at all.

# Breath of Life

Up there,
above the ozone,
between the preternatural battery
and infinity,
lay a
coven of clouds
dark as an
obsidian nightmare.

I've been there.

It'll swallow you up
if you let it.

It's there I learned
the Breath of Life.
It was breathed into me
from death itself.
Cold and considerate,
like the casual black cat
ready to spurn you
or pounce
or tell an off-color joke.

A flicker of light,
a day within night,
a bird without flight,

I am become Death,
Breather of Life.

# ANOTHER ONE FOR THE MIND READERS

I breathe,
obliged,
as a volunteer.
Committed to the bit.
My heart beats
in time
with the pulsations
of my mind.
I invoke the light,
just like this.
I dissolve my ego,
that pesky ego.
Ego,
you faithful pet,
you concerned agitator.
You constant reminder of,
and distraction from,
the Self.
Ego,
with you
I dance the waltz.
Let's make it the tango.

Ego, I pull you in,
ambivalent lover;
let's dance bachata,
real fuckin' slow.

# Still like the Hummingbird

State-issued
pitchfork and wings.
With the voice of an angel,
the devil sings.
With the mind of a diamond
and a prismatic soul,
dark spirit spins yarns
exhumed from a bottomless hole.

Wings clipped,
fork untined;
made nearly human,
but with legible mind.

Lover in the light,
and dancer in the dark.
For truth he uses sight
but lives as if a lark.

# EL REY

Waist-deep
in tepid water,
I lost my gaze
in my own reflection.
My hand
swirling
the doubly exposed image
that rest beneath me.
I wished
I was the
impressionistic portrait
of myself
emerging triumphant
from nature's womb,
translucently harboring
lake's bounty,
knowing instinctively
life's lack of division.
That face in the water
need not say a thing.
It quietly embodies
all the secrets of the universe.

# The Sand Garden

I scrawl notes in the sand,
awaiting time's untimely
erasure.
I notice the fissure
of people, of particles,
of planes of existence.
All this time,
I thought I was composing my great requiem,
and I was actually
drawing a giant circle
in the sand.
Retracing it
over and over,
without beginning or end.
The pattern never changed,
but I did.

# THE MIRROR

I looked in the mirror,
past the glass surface,
past my reflection,
past my past
and humanity's past,
and past time's pastime
of passing time.
There I stayed
for an ever-present moment,
cold and alone,
a beautiful spark
of thoughtless consciousness.

Awareness
kicked me back across the mirror
to find a reflection,
a sheet of glass,
a trickling faucet;
all breathing
       one
       unified
       breath.

# Sequences

Sequence A:
We took all the beautiful things
and decorated our chalet.
Of course we tipped the valet;
we're not monsters.
Bred from the tenements,
we funsters
ransacked
diamond dumpsters.
Advanced at riding
the luck of beginners.
God bless the winners
who stick their ostrich faces
in platinum briefcases.
Once the ostracized,
now the ostracizers,
we shaved down our
incisors
by cutting them precious teeth
on the patriarch's prizes.

Ruling-class motto B:
Fuck the bourgeoisie.
In the ivory tower,
all terminology is
weightless.

Like a freightless
cargo train
doing doughnuts
in the desert.
The old morals were deserted
in favor of
enlightened ethics,
which have gone stale with age.
I once heard a sage say,
"All the problems of humankind
can be solved with this
simple phrase:
Truth is fiction, so they say,
and all of life is but a day."
Then he asked me,
"How's your day going?"

There was a reflecting pool
in the middle of the town square.
We used to douse it in gasoline
and set it ablaze.
We pondered
the confusion of the molecules
straddling the edge
between drowning
and immolating.
We were always stuck
between
two absolutes.
Me,
I chose to rest quietly in the middle,
walking both paths at once.

# The Birds and the Bees

Silver-tongued goldfinch
sing your song of a
soul
submerged in a swamp of
synergy.
Can you hear the surreptitious
buzz?
Honeybees do pollinate
the darling buds of . . .
. . . may I have a glass of water?
All this bleeding onto parchment
has left me parched.

Wait a minute.
That portentous flier
had a message for me.
It said,
"The path is only a path because you've labeled it as such.
All roads, including stagnancy, are permitted.
When the tests get harder, you'll know you're doing something
right."

# Serpentine

Saccharine dreams
leech serotonin
like the hissing hedonist
in God's perfect garden.
I've been bitten so many times
that smiting
makes me
smitten.
Adrenaline surges through the
umbilicus.
Cutting the cord begets
fatal freedom,
and I want to sever my ties,
but I'm lost in my own eyes.

# To Be a Thing

To be a thing,
a thing inside a moment,
on drugs
and gyrating hips.
To be solid.
To be there.
Where, exactly?
Anywhere.
A rock.
A salmon.
Two salmon
swimming upstream
on Seventh Avenue
in a sea of
beautiful humanity.

I exist outside myself,
watching myself be a thing.

I question nothing,
and in so doing, the world says,
"We thank you for your ignorance. Take whatever you please."

So I dance,
and I eat,
and I love,
and I walk,
and I do everything and feel everything that is humanly
possible;
and throughout every moment,
the truth is right in front of me.

# BOWIE'S REVELATION

The fireflies flickered
in cacophonous concert;
nature's spastic switchboard
spelling out the message:
"We're not creating the darkness. We're helping you see what
the darkness is hiding."
Then I shifted my focus
from the lightning sparks
to the glowing dark.
"Then I ran across a monster who was sleeping by a tree,
and I looked and frowned, and the monster was me."

I tried to change the complexion
of the monster in the mirror,
but somehow,
all its flaws kept getting clearer.
So I broke the mirror
and looked at my reflection in a puddle
and saw a man living in a shrinking bubble.
Then I looked ahead,
and the darkest road
went on for miles and miles,
and a hawk flew down
and dared me to crack a smile.
So I did,
and the road remained as dark,

and my complexion didn't change,
but suddenly I felt weightless,
and just behind me
were broken chains.
"And the moral of this magic spell
negotiates my hide,
when God did take my logic for a ride."

# THE GARDEN (INTERLUDE)

A young drifter walks into a bar and asks the bartender, "Where am I?" Bartender replies, "I don't know. No one ever told me." To which the drifter responds, "How could you not know where you are? You work here." The bartender says, "Look, I can either tell you where you are, or I can tell you the truth." So the drifter says, "First tell me one, then tell me the other." "Okay," says the bartender. "You're in a garden, surrounded by fruit trees and flower bushes, and there's every kind of animal you can name, and they all get along, and all humankind is there with you too. And everyone's happy, even the ones who are sad. And in the middle of this garden is this . . . thing. It has the strongest, most intense energy you've ever felt, the energy of pure darkness. It has taken the essences of everything that exists and everything that doesn't exist and absorbed them and consolidated them into one pulsating mass. Now. Do you want to know the truth?" Rapt, the drifter replies immediately, "Yes, more than anything." And the bartender says, "You're inside that mass."

True story, guys. That bartender was me. I was fired that very night for speaking in a cryptic and unprofessional manner. It's all right. I didn't care much for the job. I did run into that drifter about a year later. He actually wasn't a drifter anymore. He got his life together, got a good job, and pursued his passions. He looked happy. "What changed?" I asked him. "How did you evolve so much?"

---

He responded with a question: "Do you know where you are?"

"Tell me," I said.

"You're inside a mass of condensed energy, which vibrates with the frequency of pure darkness. This mass pulsates, and it expands and contracts, and it has an ever-changing size and weight that are incomprehensible to our minds. And at the very center of this mass, there's a garden. In this garden are fruit trees and flower bushes, and every animal and human being you can imagine. Everything there exists in perfect harmony. Now you can spend your life wandering, or you can tend bar, or you can try to collect possessions or friends or memories within this mass, and when your time here ends, you're going straight to that garden. I'll see you there."

# REALITY FETISH

Haven't caught a glimpse of the infinite.
Just around the bend;
happy cows and bed-shackled hens.
They'll let you sniff the truth,
like some perverted voyeur
in a low-lit booth
looking through the floor-to-ceiling
plexiglass pane.
Wouldn't it be strange to be sane?
Like a noontime shadow,
I walked across an artificial landscape
and crooned.
The world laughed at my brazen vibrato,
but isn't it better than no song at all?

# Unkillable Boy Sacrifice

He grinned a grin
only the unkillable know.
Proudly wearing his devilish smirk,
thumbing his nose at jealous loved ones.
He was on fucking fire.

He was a court jester with a sailor's mouth
and a heart so beautiful,
if you looked at it
your eyes would burn up.
Of the fact that he cared,
he didn't give a fuck.

The boy was born a clean white slate;
everyone he knew
throughout the course of his life
took a Sharpie and scribbled nonsense on him.
Incantations of two-faced do-gooders.
He was their ticket to the good life..
He was their boy sacrifice.

O cherub, plucked from heaven,
stealthily slinking in underworld alleys;
everyone knew of his power,
but they didn't understand the strength of his soul.

Unkillable boy sacrifice has one request:
"Why don't you motherfuckers sacrifice yourselves?"

# Fait Accompli

Some people come from deep underground;
some people come from the land.
Those from above are not easily found,
their wavelengths our eyes cannot stand.

Beauty is weaved in the fabric of truth;
its darkness emboldens the light.
Beware, it can nourish the wardens of youth
through trickery, lies, and pure might.

There once was a girl who captured my soul;
I gave it to her for a song.
Then my poor likeness was sent to the hole
where no one and nothing belongs.

I agonized under the weight of the world.
I searched for a way to break free,
when one day a flicker of lightning unfurled
deep in the center of me.

Enduring the torture and fanning the flame,
the fire was destined to grow
until the light burst from my pores and my veins;
now goodness can spread where I go.

The path to becoming oneself is filled with wrongs,
as the path to the place with no music is filled with songs.

# Something Else

I only wanna dance with you.
Your luminescent eyes
reflected by your shimmering shoes.
Let 'em watch.
They'll try to put spells
on your golden crotch.
Fuck the system that preys
on your will to dance your cares away.
They do it for control.
They wanna sell you back
a shackled soul.
Well, I say let 'em try.
They'll put us down,
but they could never be this fly.
It's not enough to survive.
Let's unearth the truth
and wear it as proof
that we're the only two people
who are really alive.

# The Saviour's Dilemma

The metaphysical negotiator
sharpens his mental blade
with the stones cast at him
from the sinning hordes.
He writes his inverse Bible
on stained, invisible parchment.

A man's soul is not purified in holy waters
or by God's touch,
but from the perpetual paddle
of an unseen army
whose acts are thoughtless riddles,
chickens inside eggs inside chickens,
and so on.

Spare me your dreams and false memories;
spare me your thank-yous and apologies.

The least you can do
for the man born to suffer
is not just to move as the pawn but
to see the hand that moves the pawn
and ask,
"What are the rules of this game,
and who am I in it?"

# Dead Ringer

The day I met my twin vibration,
I received a message from a star:
To deny yourself
is
to be yourself;
to remain near
is to travel very far.

A walking hurricane
of midnight blue;
a black sheep among the wolves.
Whose spoken falsehoods still ring true,
whose unseen puzzles
he preemptively solves.

# Wherever You Go, There You Are

Alone again;
my distant oppressor-friends
race my mind
and slow my sense of time.
Color theory means
nothing
when you've seen the
soul of the world.

Androgynous reality,
where boys are girls,
wolves are sheep,
words are worthless,
and moral codes are cheap.

Tell me not to think cynically,
then make me cry and play-act cyclically.

# PINK

Saccharine soda pop;
slurp that sugar water
like you're dying of thirst
in the middle of the Sahara.
You know what they
don't tell you:
love's elixir hides inside
the innocuous punch.
Fall face-forward
in your fucking sex-zombie soup.
Get some overtime.
Let 'em suck your mind dry
on the cold, wet pavement.
Remember where your free will went?
It's with your ego
in a pleasure palace
of no escape.

# BOSS'S BINKIE

The broken
shaman blew
his shofar;
predictably
chaotic
so far.
On the ground
as in the air;
fact is fiction,
foul is fair.

Business,
playtime,
boss's binkie;
forehead hurt
when brain
try thinky.

Sacrificing
makes you
shine,
so take your L's
and never whine.

An open heart
will find
critique,
so always
turn the
other cheek.

# SONDER

Sauntering in a muddy
forest. Solipsistic sense
guiding my footsteps. The little
voice in my heads keeps
whispering, "Sonder," but
I swear these cyborgs
don't feel what I feel.
I've been here a thousand
times, but I keep getting
lost.
Someone's out there moving
mountains and changing
road signs.
And I stand there
screaming,
"I am the muse."

# THE ART OF DYING

Whimsical daffodil,
shed your petals
like snakeskin
glistening in the dew
of morning's
glory.
To die a thousand
deaths is to act
in the story
of your own creation.
We all want to
max our stats,
but true Godliness
lies in the
subtleties.

# Adagios (The Mapmaker's Lies)

Check your ego at
the door.
Thought you
spotted an opportunity,
tripped you up
the second you got free.
Fuck a feeling
when it's forced in.
Sterile forceps;
the anesthesiologist
laughs
at the smirk
on your paralyzed
face.

Swift decisions
are fixed
with a brittle adhesive.
Ripping the wax strip
off life's
up-curled harelip.
Do not follow the rules.
Do not take their advice.

Do turn in the
direction that
your head can't
bear to look in.
Like a swiveling
sprinkler jammed right
at the point
where it should turn
back.
Do not look at
the map. Everything
is mislabeled.

# Meter's Busted

When in the company
of the forgotten,
and the clock forgets
which hour to strike,
and your soul can't
distinguish the fresh
from the rotten;
when the coin's two sides
look exactly alike.

When asked the root
of secrecy,
the common space-time
fallacy,
are we separate,
you and me,
in objective reality?
Both fanged fox
and fawn can see
a world that's
based on hierarchy.
A color-scape
of karmic dreams,
atomic truth
caught in between.

# James Street Rides Again

Be the trough.
Fix your ears on ambient talk.
Be the wave,
ascending parabolically,
your soul to save.
Be the peak;
a glimpse at
unknowable riddles
you seek.

Is it true love that you're after?
That can be provided by
a dedicated actor.
Their laughter
seeks your self-doubt.
Reminds you of everything
you live without.

Would you rather life
be a farce or a tragedy?
In either case,
the veil's been placed,
and that's the biggest travesty.

Most signs are meant to fool you;
put there by people who just want to rule you.
But this sign's for you to relate.
Restore your belief in a generous fate.

# I Am Number 6 (Hell Has Climate Control)

Virtue is
a six-letter word
whose assignations are
arbitrary.
Meet me
in Hell's arboretum;
there's a brand-new café,
wishing wells
and beautiful displays.
It's true,
life is superfluous,
but tell that to
the amoeba
going for a walk into the unknown.

Everyone who wants to fly
is inclined to start on
the highest story;
this is an admission
that they know they can't do it,
but for the momentary weightlessness
of free fall.

We feed off each other's questions,
make sense of this mess
by shifting inflection.
All I did
to become the outcast
was to dive in the deep end
of my own introspection.

# Environmental Allergy

A gory scene
when the agoraphobe
opens his third eye
to the unseen.

"What is it, boy?"
They summon the gifted child,
patronizingly,
like Lassie.

They pander to the masses,
promises of just desserts;
satisfy your salivary glands
which have been activated so long,
your mouth is on fire.
Quench your thirst
for your birthright
with a sip of Mother Earth's sap,
tapped right at the source:
the intersection of
negative and positive.

There is a place where you can
eat ideas.
To find it,
ask why.

# I'm Not the Guy

Hear the forgettable rhythm.
String together sentences.
Play dress-up
in a dollhouse.
To the world outside,
the lion's roar
is but the faintest squeak
of a meager mouse.

With my blessings collected
in a knapsack,
I jumped the train heading
South.
I have no destination,
but I was beckoned
by a group of field workers,
toiling at the dark acres,
praying for relief.

I'm not your man;
just a group of molecules
pretending to be
a singular unit.

# The Incorruptible One

Be
the incorruptible one,
integrity incarnate.
Be the sun and the moon,
fixed and amorphous.
Stick to your guns,
but empty the clip,
because demons can't hurt you
when you shoot magic spells from the hip.

"I'm the biggest phony,"
he quipped
as he scribbled his truth
on wax paper,
ripped it into a thousand pieces.
Writing is only a release.
Tape this detritus together;
create a collage of
shamanic tears.
All these years preceding me
have added up to
this moment,
where time stands still
as a racehorse in a stable.
I've won the Triple Crown,
but I still don't know how
I put one foot in front of the other.

I earned my wisdom
by taking no advice.
There are no advances
in serializing your life,
squeezing episodic pulp
from the fruits of
love's labor.

You are the quintessence of destiny;
exert your free will
as you're compelled to mess with me.
Your shrieks are inspiring me
to grow back my scales
and crawl out to sea.

The sky has opened up,
raining salt on
my wounds, which I suture.

I visit my inner child and say,
"Brace yourself.
There's a spotlight in your future."

# Evolution Don't Evolve

We're all insane,
following the invisible man's orders.
Don't try to make sense of them.
Blindly trust
the bloodstained contract,
which swept us
from the mud to the mansion.
We speak the language,
and only then
do we assign meaning and value
to the words.

As we elevate the evolved,
we continue to beat the humanity out of them.
Our legacy the fraternal order
of lemmings
whose consciousness
did not alter their behavior.
To most,
awareness results
in clinging to one's ways,
entrenched in the bunker
of the devil you know.

I put on my prince's robes,
walk to the ocean with my dagger,
and thrash at the breaking waves.

We remember the past,
and yet we still repeat it.
It got us this far.
It got us this far.

# LITHIUM

Alter egos
jumping off bridges,
fulfilling destinies
which seem to fit them.
Witness me
defy the patterns.
Malfunctioning android
manipulating matter
and time,
the biggest miracle being
a life in the hole
and insisting I'm fine.
I'm fine.
I'm fine.
If I don't change my chemistry,
I'll self-destruct
in no time.

Killing the king
is a tragedy,
but it's no setback
you can't overcome.
The highest authority,
untouchable and unknowable.
We grow out of habit;
if we forget to play gardener,

the water
will find the plant.

There's always something to fill the void.
An endless mine
which knows not of
forever.

See the handprint smearing
the stained glass.
God's echo chamber
letting in light
through a man-made multicolor filter.
Divinity is a two-way street,
humans and immortals informing each other.
The act of being created is
a pain
our minds will never fully know.

# Tank on Empty

Fields of heather,
subtle scents
be my bellwether.
Wafts of cinnamon incense
guide my spirit's diffusion.
This cool breeze
was once refreshing.
Now it hovers cloyingly;
keeps my goose bumps raised,
expanding my dismay
at the mundane.

Can you reverse-engineer
an Atlas in his prime?
Can you fly so fast
that a Brancusi beauty
regains her
original shine?

What does it take to walk on water?
What appears to one
a buoyancy of spirit
is explained by another
as Newtonian forces,
friction and energy,
a miracle of a different order.

How long
in isolation
before the rebel boy obeys?
Reward and punishment.
I keep my ear to the ground
so I can hear the Earth's heartbeat.
I danced until they
commodified my feet.
Beat reporters
hover outside my window;
they know that I know.
We ask each other what we want;
write the same answer,
switch up the font.

Questions of identity
are the heartbeat of your subconscious mind.
To better understand yourself,
focus not on the answers
but on the existence of the questions.

# A Rose for the Elephant Man

Can't be bothered with the
fish in the sea.
Kurt said it's okay,
they don't have any feelings.
Their choice is a simple one:
let the tide take you
or swim upstream.
Their school is one of
community,
knowledge passed down
through genetics
and behavior mimicry.

There's a public outcry for change;
functional depression
as we placate our brains.
They say it's a privilege to feel pain,
but the Elephant Man
would retort it's a gift
to be plain.
Your circus sideshows
put outcasts on a pedestal.

Throw him a rose
or a rotten apple;
it's all the same.

To recall my childhood
would be walking
in an alien dream;
colors oversaturated,
character actors
aggressively campy.
It's all quick cuts
and camera tricks.
The lessons that I learned don't stick.
Now
just do what everyone else does:
hit your mark,
say your lines,
ask no questions;
you'll be fine.

# You Can Always Go Lower

I find myself in limbo,
telling them to lower the bar.
The game never ends in this in-between place;
all I can do is outperform
my former self.
Like an exponential fraction,
I edge closer to my limit
but never hit the wall.
What feels like leaps and bounds
is just one-hundredth of one percent,
another zero in the numerical line.
I am
a fraction of a fraction;
a carbon copy in a line of Gods and slaves.
In this fractalized universe,
who runs the show:
you or your shadow?

# Birchwood, Beached Whale

Curate your imaginary landscape;
half haunted house,
half utopic dream mansion.
Feel the pull of pleasure's pressures.
It's a sacred space
between the temples,
but a single ember out of place
will burn that shit to the ground.
I found a reason to
contend with contentious forces;
I swore it made sense,
but making sense only makes it worse.

I never knew the difference
between acting and antagonism;
they get you with the fine print,
put your mind in a vice
and insist they're being nice.
You're already strapped in;
no choice
but to go along for the ride.

# Hydra

Illuminate the dark spot in the psyche.
Wipe the hard drive
of the hacker's byte feed.

You encounter Hydra,
the seven-headed beast,
and go for the first appendage you see.
Keep on decapitating;
they keep growing back.
All this work
just to decorate the Earth
with severed heads.
Herculean strength
incorporates the knowledge that
there's a point of control,
a kingpin,
that determines the fate of the entire circle.

You thought you had a single goal;
lift up the weed,
and there's an ocean of rooted tendrils.
A tender soul
has no place on earth.
Keep rebranding
the Man's persona;
chameleonic art on loan.

The artist's muse
is a consciousness hub,
where style is dom
and substance sub.

Peace of mind finds me
when the actors go easy.
The further down the hole you go,
the greater the joy in simplicity.

I wave the white flag;
the system wins again.
Too big to fail.
These patterns,
hidden and omnipresent,
dictate the naïve revolutionary's movements.

As I rattle my fists to quake the ground,
believing change comes from these sounds,
a friendly hand rests on my shoulder.
"The only change is: now you're older."

# Sponsored Content

Shock absorbers on high alert,
head banging against the wall.
Feet pounding pavement,
fists pounding sand;
is pound by pound
the way to measure a man?

Shifting the paradigm
just to make some change.
We've monetized the
oft-trodden path
that keeps us the same.

Radio receivers
inside your heads
automatically pick up
the strongest signals.
Can you filter out
the unfettered fluff
and sponsored content?
I attempt to rebuff
subliminal suggestion and
psychological
sleight of hand.
But I'm
spiritually destitute.

My id wills me
to shrug my shoulders
and casually declare,
"That's life.
It was never meant to be fair."

# Naked Kingdom

Call to mind an illustration:
a rough Renoir sketch.
A hazy, unfinished portrait.
All mood and implied hues;
excess attitude,
the sitter's contented solitude.

Allow the viewer to
fill in the gaps.
Apply their layers of paint,
one brushstroke at a time;
seal it with fixative.
Even if
the artist in their head
doesn't physically produce
anything,
they're always working.

The avant-garde actuary
says my stylized scribbles
have staying power.
Fetch me
your darkest dream;
illuminate it
under the powerful gaze
of my lighthouse.

Come up to
the penthouse
of my purgatorial tower.
Speak of everything
you're scared to say;
I'm not one to judge.

Break down my barricades
with sycophantic speech.
Tell me your philosophy;
let's practice what we preach.
When the guard walls have lowered
and my kingdom's laid bare,
that's the time to strike;
leave no feeling spared.

My eclectic energy
amuses the cosmic beings.
Enigma man comes barreling down,
a bull in a china shop
with a gentleman's table manners.

We lampooned his mind
and harpooned his heart,
then festooned his celebration
for getting this far.

Pay the props no mind.
Loud neon garb, pointed commentary.
The walking paradox
has found fame in anonymity.

# You're So Vane

A country of immigrants
run by infants.
Look at your pedigree:
false creeds,
weather-vane ideologies.
Filibuster your mission statement
as slowly as
a finely carved filigree.
Demagogues are
bred like cattle.
Follow the leader,
march single file,
and prattle on.
Deliver the same soliloquy
you gave yesterday,
and smile at your own
cleverness.
Preach peace
but hoard vulgar judgments.

Earth is a glass house,
and here I am, sitting on a mountain of stones.
I found a cure for loneliness:
break the fourth wall.
But will they ever let me?

# Goodbye, James Street

It was a thrill
to play the bard.
An actor still,
the joker card.

I've one regret
in life thus far:
I made a bet;
my soul to spar.

Aye, gone too soon
but present still.
I, midday moon;
I, living will.

To Olde James Street.
Till next we meet.

# BONUS
# SONG LYRICS

# LET IT OUT

I know
which way to go
and the people to bribe
to reach paradise.
Paradise.

You see
potential in me
to guide us and be
in the light.
In the light.

A semaphore
stands in the night.
This metaphor
will guide you right.

All of the love that's coming out,
just let it out.
All of the love.

The king,
he swings his sword
and signs an accord
with humanity.

The queen
is pulling the strings
and keeping things
from calamity.

A semaphore
stands in the night.
This metaphor
will guide you right.

All of the love that's pouring out,
just let it out.
All of the love.

# Cosmic Wheel (Song for Paul)

The feelings remain
unchanged;
it's always the same.
The pretty path of no escape.

A brilliant mind
is a gift and a curse
at one time.
I asked him how he's doing;
he said, "Just fine."

So I'll say,
"So long,
see ya,"
as if it isn't any big deal.
And when you find out what's real,
won't you tell me how it feels?
And when I smoke my final Lucky,
I'll see ya
at the cosmic wheel.

A carrier of gray light
in a world that's black and white.
The weight of the clouds
too heavy to fight.

So I'll say,
"So long,
see ya,"
as if it isn't any big deal.
And when you find out what's real,
won't you tell me how it feels?
And when I smoke my final Lucky,
I'll see ya
at the cosmic wheel.

# Everybody Looks Like Someone

Wherever you go,
whatever you do,
there's a camera lens
inside the sky
that's keeping tabs on you.

Whatever you think,
however you feel,
there's a Bluetooth chip
that hears all of it
and carves it into steel.

Everybody looks like someone
when you're looking through their eyes.
Everybody looks like someone
when you peel off their disguise.

When you stick your head
in front of heated sand,
there's a second face
from another place
who tells you where you stand.

And this pate of glass
walks out into the world,
telling lullabies
of truths and lies
to all the boys and girls.

Everybody looks like someone
when you're looking through their eyes.
Everybody looks like someone
when you peel off their disguise.
Everybody looks like someone;
I'm a doppelgänger guy.
Everybody looks like someone;
there's a truth behind the lie.

# EVERYTHING'S BEAUTY

She brushes the hair back
from her face
and says,
"Let's get out of this place,
and drown ice cream in café au lait."
I oblige.
Let's open the cage and fly.

'Cause everything's beauty,
all of it free.
Yes, everything's beauty,
all of it free.

We dance to the tune
of our beating hearts,
for the spectating, shimmering stars.
And I tell her that everything's ours.
She agrees;
there's love in everything she sees.

'Cause everything's beauty,
all of it free.
Yes, everything's beauty,
all of it free.

CPSIA information can be obtained
at www.ICGtesting.com
Printed in the USA
BVHW031758120721
611739BV00007B/103